C000161816

TH
BOOK
OF
CREATION

ספר יצירה

THE
BOOK
OF
CREATION

Translation and Commentaries by
IRVING FRIEDMAN

SAMUEL WEISER, INC.
New York

First Printing 1977.

Copyright © 1977 Irving Friedman

Published by
Samuel Weiser, Inc.
734 Broadway
New York, N.Y. 10003

ISBN 0-87728-289-7
Library of Congress
Card Catalogue Number
76-15537

Typography by
Kenneth R. Patton
New York

Printed in the USA by
Noble Offset Printers, Inc.
New York

CONTENTS

Hebrew Letter	Hebrew Letter Name	Roman character by which expressed in this work.
א	Aleph	A
ב	Beth	B
ג	Gimel	G
ד	Daleth	D
ה	He	H
ו	Vav	V
ז	Zayin	Z
ח	Cheth	Ch
ט	Teth	T
י	Yod	Y
כ	Kaph	K
ל	Lamed	L
מ	Mem	M
נ	Nun	N
ס	Samekh	S
ע	Ayin	O
פ	Pe	P
צ	Tzaddi	Tz
ק	Qoph	Q
ר	Resh	R
ש	Shin	Sh
ת	Tau	Th

PREFACE

WE CAN IMAGINE the author of the *Book of Creation* smiling patiently at a request to justify this work. It is a book about the meaning of life and the universe, how man can approach them, and how he may even grasp their superhuman content.

The difficulty lies in linking the profound ideas expressed with the quest of man. We may well ask, "What if the universe is as the author describes it, how does it affect what man does?"

The answer to this question arises directly from the nature of the universe. There is an undeniable correspondence between man and the higher as well as lower realms. Knowing what he is enables him to choose what he shall do and even edges him a little along the road toward it.

This is certainly not a new way of appraising man's situation. Neither is it exclusively an old one. Therefore the perennial interest in this work is not merely that of scholars. It is more nearly the concern of an increasing number who cannot take the world at face value and who search for its less tangible aspects.

Some would have wished that the author had spelled out more specifically the techniques he was propounding. Commentators in later centuries have not hesitated to embroider their own with his implications, whether or not their creations were appropriate to the author's time and place.

The present translator embodies his conclusions as to the author's basic prescription in the final chapter called, "The Method of Salvation." It remains only to justify another English translation. The reason can only be to arouse further interest in this most ancient Kabbalistic work by rendering it as simply and accurately as possible.

INTRODUCTION

THE BOOK OF CREATION is surrounded by paradoxes. Throughout the centuries, it has had an influence out of all proportion to its size, leaving an indelible mark on Western thought. Yet it has somehow resisted penetration by the ordinary English-speaking public, although it has been available in that language since the middle of the nineteenth century.

The reasons are not hard to find, but they only compound the problem. There are different Hebrew versions, and later interpolations have hardly helped toward uniformity. Apparently, it was regarded highly enough to be worthy of additions, but not enough to preserve the original text. Nevertheless, despite the variations, the main thrust and message of the work remain abundantly clear.

In sharp contrast to the obscurity of other speculative works, the style of the *Book of Creation* is precise and logical to an extreme, almost as if it were a formal summary of the subject in outline form. Paradoxically, however, it contains ideas wrapped in symbolic garb which have been the subject of considerable speculation but seem to remain as impenetrable as ever.

Some of them depend on the double meaning of a Hebrew term, which is therefore impervious to translation by just one word. Some appear to be Greek in origin, while others can be understood only against the background of the cosmopolitan mentality of Alexandrian Jewry in the early Christian centuries. Included in this background were all the religious currents that cross-fertilized each other during this period, together with associated movements upon which later generations have cast a jaundiced eye, such as astrology, alchemy, magic and number-mysticism.

The synthesis by the *Book of Creation* of all this spiritual ferment is always a Judaic synthesis, but it is also undeniably a studied attempt to encompass and unify a variety of elements. These elements are so intertwined that it is often difficult to sift out what is distinctively Judaic. It would be rash to deny that this intermixture could be responsible for the varieties of Judaic thought throughout the ages and in particular for the provocative differences between the early Kabbalah of the *Book of Creation* and the later Kabbalah of the *Book of Splendor* (the *Zohar*).

For example, the Mesopotamian-Persian influence on Judaism is undeniable, supported as it is by the Biblical account of the Babylonian exile and the return to Palestine under the Persians.

The influence of the Sumerian-Babylonian culture included the epics of Creation and Flood, and their calendar. From the Persians came the doctrine of spirits of light and darkness, their system of angelology, and their concept of bodily resurrection.

The Persian Zoroastrians seem to have originated the doctrine of the elements which the Greeks later popularized and which plays so important a role in the *Book of Creation.* In the latter, air is a direct descendant of, and to a large extent indistinguishable from, the Spirit that directly represents the deity. Its role in the universe is to balance the two forces of fire and water, which may be interpreted as active and passive.

Among the ancient Mesopotamians, the god of air assumed a similar and predominant role over the gods of heaven and water. Among the Persians, the air or wind constitutes the third entity between the two spirits. It forms the substance of the creator as vital spirit maintaining the macrocosm. As breath, closely related to the soul, it also keeps the body alive.

A similar conception of air as the primary and universal substance was held by Anaximenes of the Greek naturalist school of Ionians in Asia Minor. He construed fire as rarefied air, while water and earth are condensed air. This seems to have been the view of the Pythagoreans and the Stoics as well. Aristotle, who along with Plato is the source of many of our views about the Pythagoreans, added ether as a universal substance to the four elements. The spiritual air of the *Book of Creation* has actually been translated by some as ether, and this highlights the influence that the Persian and Greek theory of the elements may have had on the *Book of Creation.*

The latter envisages its law of three as a scale balancing merit and defect. This is the same picture that we get from the Zoroastrian mean as the mediator between excess and deficiency. This concept descended through the Pythagoreans to become the Golden Mean of Aristotle.

It would be enticing to follow this first major theme of the three forces through the trinities of all the major mythologies and religions. Above all, it plays a major role in the Tree of Life of the later Kabbalah.

However, the *Book of Creation* is not just speculative. All its principles find their ultimate significance in a correspondence with the life and body of man. The passive element water, from which the earth was created, is also the substance of the abdomen of man, which can be interpreted as the seat of his instincts. The active element fire corresponds to the head. The balancing element air, kin to both the spirit and the atmosphere, is situated in man's body between his head and abdomen, being breathed through his chest. The author enlarges this chest area by using a Hebrew term for it which means trunk, or even body, just as the air in the atmosphere tends to include both the heavens and the earth.

Thus, according to the *Book of Creation,* the breath is a key element in the life-giving balance of man. In Hebrew as well as in English, "spirit," derived from the Latin *spiritus,* the soul, is inextricably intertwined with the process of respiration. The Greek *psyche* also means "to breathe" and gave rise to the concept of the breath-soul. No doubt there were similar relationships among the Persians, the Egyptians, and in other traditions.

The second major theme of the *Book of Creation* is its law of seven exhibited in the planets, days of the week, directions, divine qualities, and openings in the head. It embodies the idea of antagonism, especially in the seven pairs of contrasting qualities. Indeed, this planetary world can be called a world of unresolved opposites, which has to go outside itself to find its center of balance. There is also an order of progression implicit in the order of the planets and its derivative order of the days of the week. However, this progression is one that the reader is left to ferret out for himself from the analogies that are given.

This world of seven opposites is also one which is not lacking parallels among other traditions. Both Pythagoras and the Alexandrian Jew Philo based their universe on pairs of opposing qualities, although not restricted to seven in number. The seven Holy Immortals of the Persians seem very close in spirit to the qualities of the *Book of Creation*. Of course, the seven planets were the common heritage of the ancient world, but although the book makes them correspond to particular qualities, there is no reference to divination, in accordance with the antipathy of the Jews toward it.

The Babylonians and the Gnostics regarded the world of the planets as an evil, lower realm because it was the world of matter from which it was necessary to escape. However, neither the Jews nor the Persian Zoroastrians agreed with this attitude toward matter, which they rather felt was to be redeemed. This redemption was possible because matter, too, reflected the upper realm on a lower level.

Here also, speculation is abruptly curtailed by the embodiment of the seven in the body of man. The seven openings in his head correspond to four of his senses, and are therefore the point of entry of the outside universe into his world.

The third major theme of this work is its law of twelve, illustrated in the constellations of the Zodiac, the months of the year, the diagonal directions, the functions of man, and his limbs and organs. This law is a picture of sharp contrasts intensified to the point that they are arranged as if for war. The twelve may be arranged in four groups of three, as in the signs of the Zodiac or the seasons of the year. The contrasts of love and hate, life and death, form another basis for this classification (see chap. VI, verse 8). But the heart in the body of man seems to unify the conflict in him, just as the spatial and temporal universes are also unifications of conflict. The central unifying element of all three is called the king — on his throne, in a province, or at war.

The king on his throne or in his palace is an image of the divine aspects extensively employed in early Jewish throne or chariot mysticism. This Work of the Chariot, carried on by the Riders or Descenders in it, dealt with the attainment of ecstasy through the contemplation of God's appearance. It contrasted with the Work of Creation, the speculative branch of early Jewish mysticism. The *Book of Creation* is obviously an attempt to unify both trends.

But the non-Judaic influences are as evident in regard to the law of twelve in this work as they are in the other themes. The twelve signs of the Zodiac are a product of the Babylonian and Egyptian study of the heavens. The names of the months were adopted by the Jews from the Babylonians. The word describing the twelve directions as oblique or diagonal is itself Greek in derivation. The Pythagoreans regarded the twelve-sided solid, the dodecahedron, as the closest to the perfect sphere which is the universe, and it was therefore their symbol for wholeness.

The whole attitude of the Pythagoreans toward numbers as qualities, which they may have inherited from but certainly shared with the Egyptians, was the same idea that underlies the Judaic Sefiroth. This is the dominant theme not only of the *Book of Creation,* but in a different form, of the later Kabbalah as well. Ten in number, the Sefiroth correspond with the first ten letter-numbers of the alphabet, both letters and numbers being represented by the same characters. At the same time they represent the elements of creation, whether as substance and space in the *Book of Creation,* or as qualities of being in the later Kabbalah.

Following this dominant unity of the ten Sefiroth, there is the grand synthesis presided over by the twenty-two letters of the Hebrew alphabet, which is composed of the laws of three, seven and twelve. Each law is represented by an equivalent number of letters, and each letter corresponds to one of the facets of that Law, such as a planet, month, or part of the body.

Now, although the ten Sefiroth may be regarded as the sum of the laws of three and seven, this is not actually the picture given by our author. He does say that spirit, the first of the Sefiroth, is also the first of the letters, and he does derive both sequences from it. However, the order of the letters representing the three laws and their corresponding worlds is different from that of the alphabet. If the ten Sefiroth are to represent the worlds of the laws of three and seven, then we were hasty in calling their order that of the first ten letters of the alphabet. The *Book of Creation* actually lists the order of the Sefiroth by the names of the numbers and not by the symbols for the numbers which are identical with the letters.

Our author is evidently synthesizing two orders of letter-numbers, one based on quality and one based on numerical sequence. He may be unifying two separate streams of creation, one based on the ten Sefiroth, the other on the three laws.

Although the *Book of Creation* may have resulted from some of the formative influences recapitulated above, it became a causative influence in its turn. For example, the controversial Gnosticism which has been credited with transmitting influences from the early Middle East to become the parent of later heresies may actually have been the product of certain sects within Judaism. Its numerical symbolism, its treatment of spiritual-material elements, its angelic archons and aeons variously counted as seven and twelve are all reminiscent of the *Book of Creation*.

Among other possible effects of this work, the divinatory Tarot cards cannot be omitted. Although this precursor to our pack of playing cards is traditionally credited to the Egyptians, still a Hebrew letter is ascribed to each of the twenty-two major trumps, which match in number the letters of the Hebrew alphabet.

But perhaps the most puzzling question regarding the effects of the *Book of Creation* concerns its relation to the Kabbalah that followed almost a millenium later, in the *Zohar,* the *Book of Splendor.* The surface similarities are as bewitching as the surface differences. Both are based on ten Sefiroth of creation, but the two groups appear as far removed as the physical universe and the aesthetic qualities revered by man. Gradually, however, we see how the physical and spatial elements of the *Book of Creation* are reflected in the psychic and spiritual life of man. Working back from the divine qualities of the *Book of Splendor,* we see how they are subtly related to the physical qualities of the universe.

The earlier law of three is transformed into the triads of the later Kabbalistic Tree of Life, which themselves seem to find a later echo in Hegel. The earlier law of seven is reflected in the seven lower Sefiroth of the later Kabbalah, the Sefiroth of construction terminating in the world.

But this influence of one doctrine upon another a millenium later does not take place without subtle transformations whose inner workings are largely hidden from us. It is no wonder that some scholars have concluded that we are dealing with two distinct entities.

For example, the earlier version emphasizes a three-letter name of God YHV, which no doubt reflects its tri-partite division of the universe, and is related to the Greek Gnostic IAO, or IEU. But this has somehow become transformed by the addition of a second H into the unpronounceable Tetragrammaton, YHVH. The three elements of the *Book of Creation* thereby become transformed into the more familiar four elements. The four letters of the Great Name become stages in the development of the Sefiroth, which are symbolized by the familial terms Father, Mother, Son, Daughter that inevitably recall the Christian Trinity. The development of Tetrads of Gods out of Trinities is a familiar phenomenon in various ancient religions. It would lead one to believe that the emphasis of the *Book of Creation* on the law of three is of ancient derivation.

There are other interesting differences between the earlier and later traditions. The *Book of Creation* has a strictly deductive style wherein the world is logically derived from its primordial elements. The later *Book of Splendor* is more inductive, deriving its primordial metaphysics from the visible universe.

The luxuriance of the whole later development can hardly be regarded as implicit in the concise *Book of Creation.* But the very simplicity of the latter's principal theme somehow seems to epitomize the later blossoming. The unity of the divine is at the center of all apparent diversity, supporting and giving rise to it. This central, subterranean unity indicates the direction of man's search.

CHAPTER I

THE TEN SEFIROTH

1. In thirty-two mysterious paths of wisdom did God decree — the God of Hosts, the Living God and King of the Universe, the Almighty God, Merciful and Gracious, High and Exalted, dwelling aloft eternally, Holy in His Name. He created His universe with three numerations: Number, Speech, and Writing.

2. Ten Sefiroth alone and twenty-two foundation letters: three mothers, seven doubles, and twelve simple letters.

3. Ten Sefiroth alone: like the number of ten fingers — five against five with the one covenant in the center: the word of the tongue and the circumcision of the skin.

4. Ten Sefiroth alone: ten and not nine, ten and not eleven. Understand with wisdom and be wise with understanding. Examine with them and search among them. Know, think, and visualize. Ponder deeply and seat the Creator in His place.

5. Ten Sefiroth alone: they are measured by ten without end: the depth of the first and the depth of the last, the depth of good and the depth of evil, the depth above and the depth below, the depth of the east and the depth of the west, the depth of the north and the depth of the south. One Lord, God the Faithful King, rules them all from His Holy dwelling for all eternity.

6. Ten Sefiroth alone: their appearance is like a flash of lightning and their destination is beyond bounds. His word is in them when they go out and when they return. At His command they rush like a whirlwind and bow down before His throne.

7. Ten Sefiroth alone: their end is linked to their beginning and their beginning to their end, as the flame is linked to the burning coal. Know, think, and visualize that the Lord is one without a second, and before one what do you count?

8. Ten Sefiroth alone: restrain your mouth from speaking and your heart from thinking. And if your mouth races to speak and your heart to think, return to the place about which it is written: "And the living creatures rushed out and returned." On this the covenant was made.

9. Ten Sefiroth alone:

One: The spirit of the living God, blessed and praised be the name of the living One of the universes. Voice, spirit, and word are the holy spirit.

Two: He ordained spirit from spirit. And he hewed from it twenty-two foundation letters — three mothers, seven doubles and twelve simple letters. And spirit is the first of them.

Three: He ordained water from spirit. And He hewed from them the formless and the void, mud and clay. He ordained them like a garden bed. He arranged them like a wall. He interwove them like a fortification. He poured snow on them and it became dust, as it is said, "He saith to the snow, be thou the earth."

Four: He ordained fire from water. And he hewed from it the throne of glory; Serafim, Ofanim, and the Holy Animals and the Ministering Angels. And with these three he founded his dwelling, as it is said: "He maketh His angels spirits, His ministers a flaming fire." He chose three of the simple letters by the secret of the three mothers אמש. He fixed them in His Great Name and sealed six extremities with them.

Five: He sealed height. He turned upward and sealed it with יהו .

Six: He sealed depth. He turned downward and sealed it with יוה .

Seven: He sealed east. He turned forward and sealed it with היו .

Eight: He sealed west. He turned backward and sealed it with הוי .

Nine: He sealed south. He turned right and sealed it with ויה .

Ten: He sealed north. He turned left and sealed it with והי .

10. These are the ten Sefiroth alone: One spirit of the living God, spirit from spirit, water from spirit, fire from water, height and depth, east and west, south and north.

LANGUAGE NOTES

VERSE

1. Various Hebrew terms are rendered here by "God": *Yah* (יָה), YHVH (יְהוָה), *Elohim* (אֱלֹהִים), and its singular *El* (אֵל). Although one translation renders *numerations* as "forms of expression," its root is exactly the same as that of the three words translated as *Number* (*sfar* סְפָר), *Speech* (*Sippur* ספּור), and *Writing* (*safer* סֵפֶר).

2. *Sefiroth* (סְפִירוֹת) probably is also derived from the same root, appearing to be the feminine plural while *numerations* (*Sefarim* סְפָרִים) is a masculine plural. However, other derivations have been suggested for *Sefiroth*. It conveys the rich meaning of numbered qualities or elements of God and the universe. See comments on *Sefiroth* below.

The Hebrew term for *alone* is *Belimah* (בְּלִימָה) and is used to characterize the ten Sefiroth throughout this chapter. Literally, it means "without what" from which some have derived "out of nothing." It also signifies physical restraint, and this connotation is particularly appropriate to verse 8, which relates the Sefiroth to restraint in speaking and thinking. However, the other paragraphs suggest unity, energy, clarity, infinity, and restriction in number.

3. The Hebrew term *Milah* (מִלָה) is the same for both *word* and *circumcision,* pointing up the analogy drawn between the two covenants. They are both central to man in this verse, and the idea of the center is the veiled theme of this entire work.

4. The literal meaning of the phrase translated as *ponder deeply* is "Stand something in its pit" (or "clarify"). Its obvious meaning is that a deep search will bring one closer to the divine.

Know, think, and visualize do not appear in all versions.

5. *Depth* is the literal translation of *Omek* (עוֹמֶק). However, others have translated it here as dimension, infinity, and principle. The word translated as *measured* also conveys the meaning of attribute.

8. Ezekiel I:14.

9. In translating the words *spirit* and *air,* I have
accepted the interpretation that the first derivation of
spirit is also spirit and that air becomes differentiated
from it only in the later stage described in Chapter III.
Other interpretations derive air from spirit at this point,
although the same word is used here for both: *Ruach*
(רוח), which also means wind, or breath. The word for air
is *Avir* (אֲוִיר), which may also be related to the word for
light, *Aur* (אוֹר). The text also uses the two in combination as *Avir Ruach,* air of spirit, spiritual air, and some
have used "ether" as a synonym.

 The formless and the void are the Biblical *Tohu* (תֹהוּ)
and *Bohu* (בֹהוּ) of Genesis.

 The *twenty-two letters* are here derived from spirit
just as the elements are, separately. They are arranged in
layers, like a fortified wall.

 Earth is not a separate element but is derived from
water through snow (see Job. XXXVII:6).

 Fire is an original element derived from water, yet
fire supports water in Chapter VI.

 The phrase *throne of glory* is the vision of God in the
earliest Jewish throne-mysticism, embodying all creation, and tracing back to Ezekiel and the apocryphal *Book
of Enoch,* as do the following terms.

 The *Serafim* (שְׂרָפִים)are one of the highest orders of
angels, whose name is related to burning and the serpent.

 The *Ofanim* (אוֹפַנִים) are the wheels or angelic energies. The *Holy animals* (*Hayoth* חַיּוֹת) are the four
Cherubim that support the throne, the living creatures of
verse 8, uniting the forms of man, lion, ox, and eagle.

 *He maketh His angels spirits, His ministers a flaming
fire* is quoted from Psalms 104:4.

 The *Great Name* is the Tetragrammaton or Ineffable
name: YHVH (יהוה). This name exists independently of
the three simple letters chosen to represent it, perhaps
being of the nature of God Himself. The three letters
vary in order, to fit the different dimensions and directions. The dimensions are called extremities, perhaps to
indicate that this process of sealing restricts their infinite
extension.

CHAPTER II

THE TWENTY-TWO LETTERS

1. Twenty-two foundation letters: three mothers, seven doubles, and twelve simple letters. Three mothers א מ ש ; their foundation is the scale of merit and defect, with the tongue ordained to balance the two. Three mothers א מ ש : מ is silent, ש is sibilant, א is the air of the spirit that balances the two.

2. Twenty-two foundation letters: He ordained them, He hewed them, He combined them, He weighed them, He interchanged them. And He created with them the whole creation and everything to be created in the future.

3. Twenty-two foundation letters: He ordained them by voice, He hewed them from spirit, He fixed them in the mouth at five places: the letters א ה ח ע in the throat, ג י כ ק at the palate, ד ט ל נ ת on the tongue, ז ש ס ר צ at the teeth, ב ו מ פ at the lips.

4. Twenty-two foundation letters: He fixed them on a wheel like a wall with 231 gates and He turns the wheel forward and backward. As a sign of this there is no good higher than joy (ע נ ג) and there is no evil worse than affliction (נ ג ע).

5. How did He combine, weigh, and interchange them? א with all and all with א; ב with all and all with ב; and so on each in turn. There are 231 gates. And all creation and all language come from one name.

6. He created substance from the formless and made nothing into something. He hewed great pillars from intangible air. This is a sign that א combines with all and all with א. He looked and He spoke and He made all creation and all language from one name. A sign of it is the twenty-two inclinations in one body.

LANGUAGE NOTES

VERSE

1. The Hebrew word *Lashon* (לָשׁוֹן) which I have translated as *tongue,* can also mean the pointer indicating the balance on the scale. It is related by speech to air which balances the two other mother letters differentiated by volume of sound. These two letters Sh (שׁ) and M (מ) appear on the scale as merit and defect, morally as well as physically.

2. These are the operations by which the letters become agents of creation throughout the book:

ordain, decree, or inscribe— from Hebrew *Chakok* (חָקֹק).

hew or form — from Hebrew *Chatsov* (חָצֹב).

combine, purify — from Hebrew *Tsarof* (צָרֹף).

weigh — from Hebrew *Shakol* (שָׁקֹל).

interchange — from Hebrew *Hamor* (חָמֹר.)

3. The linguistics of this classification reveal a penetrating analysis by the author.

4 and 5. The 231 gates represent the number of possible combinations of the twenty-two Hebrew letters by twos. This seems to support the theory that the original Hebrew roots were of two letters, as against their later development into three-letter roots. 231 is the product of 3, 7, and 11.

The text seems to imply a circular wall, with each two-letter combination as a gate, the whole wall rotating as a wheel. Since the wheel can rotate in either direction, the combination of letters can be forward or backward. Thus the Hebrew words for joy and affliction consist of the same letters, but reversed (עֹנֶג) and (נֶגַע). The name of the planet Venus is *Nogah* (נוֹגַה), possibly related to affliction from the time when all planets were considered unlucky.

6. Just as the letter A (א) combines with all other letters, so its analogue, air of spirit (or ether) is the source of and combines with the material world, including the body of man. In the final sentence, the last two words mean either "in one body" or "in the body of א", which again links the corporeal with the spiritual.

CHAPTER III

THE LAW OF THREE

1. Three mothers אמש their foundation is the scale of merit and defect with the tongue ordained to balance the two.

2. Three mothers אמש: a great secret, mysterious, concealed and sealed by six rings. From them came forth fire, water, and spirit, differentiated into masculine and feminine. Three mothers אמש, from whom were born three fathers, and from the fathers everything was created.

3. Three mothers אמש: He ordained them, hewed them, combined them, weighed them, and interchanged them. And He sealed with them three mothers אמש in the universe, three mothers אמש in the year, and three mothers אמש in the male and female person.

4. Three mothers אמש in the universe: spirit, water, and fire. Heaven was created from fire, earth was created from water, and air created from spirit balances the two.

5. Three mothers אמש in the year: heat, cold, and abundance. Heat was created from fire, cold was created from water, and abundance created from spirit balances the two.

6. Three mothers אמש in the person: head, abdomen, and body. Head was created from fire, abdomen was created from water, and body from spirit balances the two.

7. He enthroned the letter א in spirit, bound a crown upon it, and fused them together. He sealed with them air in the universe, abundance in the year and body in the person — the male with אמש and the female with אשמ.

8. He enthroned the letter מ in water, bound a crown upon it, and fused them together. He sealed with them earth in the universe, cold in the year, and abdomen in the person — the male with מאש and the female with משא.

9. He enthroned the letter ש in fire, bound a crown upon it, and fused them together. He sealed with them heaven in the universe, heat in the year, and head in the person.

LANGUAGE NOTES

VERSE

2. The *great secret* of the three mothers is mentioned in chapter I, where it was the basis for the choice of the three letters YHV (יהו) constituting God's name and their use in varying modes to seal the six directions.

We have just been told that the foundation of the three mothers is a scale whose two ends convey the meaning of high and low quality, fullness and lack, positive and negative. Now the differentiation into male and female is mentioned, which was not referred to in chapters I or II. The law of three is always called the mothers, but here the three fathers are introduced, without a clear indication of what they refer to, except that they come from the mothers. While the later Kabbalah makes extensive use of the concept of father, here it seems to be an insertion in an otherwise feminine hierarchy, except that the fathers give rise to the offspring.

3. Some versions employ "create" in verses 3, 7, 8, and 9, instead of "seal," as I have done. In addition, this work draws a distinction between two types of creation not too readily transferable to English. The word *Baro* (בְּרָא) is usually used for creation in a higher world, out of nothing. The word *Yatsor* (יָצֹר) is employed for creation in a lower world, from pre-existing elements, and the title of this book is derived from it. However, *Baro* is also used extensively by the author, showing that he is giving "creation" a broad meaning. Therefore, the more restricted term "formation" is not used here to translate the title, as some have employed it. The author's universe of creation is spread throughout space, time, and man.

4. Here again earth is derived from water as its representative in the universe.

5. The threefold division of time is based on the seasons, which are here construed as three in number, not four. The heat-cold classification is alchemical, based on the system of the ancient Greeks. The division of the spatial universe is based on the alchemical dry-moist classification. *Reviyah* (רְוִיָה) connotes abundance, both as to temperature and as to moisture.

6. Most translators render the human representative of spirit or air as chest. However, the Hebrew

Geviyah (גְּוִיָּה) means body, or the trunk as its main section. The whole body would therefore be the balancing element between the head and belly elements.

7. All three Hebrew words for the representatives of air-spirit have some similarities in the letters they contain and therefore in their pronunciation: *Avir* (אַוִּיר) for air, *Reviyah* (רְוִיָּה) for abundance, and *Geviyah* (גְּוִיָּה) for body or trunk.

To give a letter dominion over an element, a crown is bound upon it and fused to it. This may refer to its royal sanctification or even to the upper element of the square Hebrew letters.

8. The author attempts to relate the variation in male and female with a different order of letters as to spirit, A (א); and water, M (מ); but none is attempted for fire, Sh (ש). In both cases the word embodying the feminine order has a negative connotation: A Sh M (אשם) meaning guilt or desolation, M Sh A (מ ש א) meaning burden or debt.

CHAPTER IV

THE LAW OF SEVEN

1. Seven double letters בגדכפרת : their foundation is life, well-being, wisdom, wealth, beauty, fruitfulness, and dominion.

2. Seven doubles בגד כפרת that are pronounced in two ways: in a pattern of soft and hard, strong and weak.

3. Seven doubles בגדכפרת in pronunciation and in opposition: the opposite of life is death; the opposite of well-being is misfortune; the opposite of wisdom is folly; the opposite of wealth is poverty; the opposite of beauty is ugliness; the opposite of fruitfulness is barrenness; the opposite of dominion is servitude.

4. Seven doubles בגדכפרת corresponding to the seven extremities: the extremities of above and below, east and west, north and south; and the holy palace in the center sustaining them all.

5. Seven doubles בגדכפרת : seven and not six, seven and not eight. Examine with them and search among them. Ponder deeply and seat the Creator in His place.

6. Seven doubles בגדכפרת : He ordained them, hewed them, combined them, and interchanged them. And He created with them seven planets in the universe, seven days in the year, and seven gateways in the male and female person.

7. Seven planets in the universe: Saturn, Jupiter, Mars, Sun, Venus, Mercury, Moon. Seven days in the year: the seven days of the week. Seven gateways in the male and female person: two eyes, two ears, two nostrils, and the mouth.

8. He enthroned the letter ב in Life, bound a crown upon it, and fused them together. He created with them Saturn in the universe, the first day in the year, and the right eye in the male and female person.

9. He enthroned the letter ג in well-being, bound a crown upon it, and fused them together. He created with them Jupiter in the universe, the second day in the year, and the left eye in the male and female person.

10. He enthroned the letter ד in wisdom, bound a crown upon it, and fused them together. He created with

them Mars in the universe, the third day in the year and the right ear in the male and female person.

11. He enthroned the letter כ in wealth, bound a crown upon it, and fused them together. He created with them the Sun in the universe, the fourth day in the year, and the left ear in the male and female person.

12. He enthroned the letter פ in beauty, bound a crown upon it, and fused them together. He created with them Venus in the universe, the fifth day in the year, and the right nostril in the male and female person.

13. He enthroned the letter ר in fruitfulness, bound a crown upon it, and fused them together. He created with them Mercury in the universe, the sixth day in the year, and the left nostril in the male and female person.

14. He enthroned the letter ת in dominion, bound a crown upon it, and fused them together. He created with them the Moon in the universe, the seventh day of the year, and the mouth in the male and female person.

15. Seven doubles ב ג ד כ פ רת with which were ordained seven universes, seven firmaments, seven earths, seven seas, seven rivers, seven deserts, seven days, seven weeks, seven years, seven sabbatical years, seven jubilees. Therefore He loves the sevens in everything under the heavens.

16. How did He combine them? Two stones build two houses, three stones build six houses, four stones build twenty-four houses, five stones build a hundred and twenty houses, six stones build seven hundred and twenty houses, seven stones build five thousand and forty houses. Begin from here and think of what the mouth is unable to say and the ear is unable to hear.

LANGUAGE NOTES

VERSE

1. The word *foundation* (Hebrew *Yesodan* יְסוֹדָן), qualifying the seven and later the twelve letters, is used in certain versions and not in others. It has been interpreted by some as characterizing the letters as being elemental, i.e. the elements out of which the material universe is built. Otherwise, it may refer to the inherent quality associated with a particular number, or may simply be translated as "He appointed them."

2. Today we recognize a difference in pronunciation for only four letters: B and V (ב & בּ), K and Ch (כּ & כ), P and F (פּ & פ), Th and S (תּ & ת). However, the dot placed in the center to mark hard letters is still used for G and D (ד & ג) in certain countries.

3. The twofold pronunciation symbolizes the opposition of the qualities. The quality here rendered as *well-being* is usually translated as "peace" (*Shalom* שָׁלוֹם). However, its opposite quality in most versions of this chapter appears as *misfortune* (*Roah* רַע), which makes more sense when opposed to well-being.

4. It is not indicated which directions apply to which letters, although the implication is that they should be taken in order. It is also not clear whether the *holy palace in the center* refers to the central letter K (כ), the first letter B (ב), or the last letter Th (ת). In chapter VI the seven are described as three against three with one, the balance, between them.

5. This is the same language as used in chapter I to describe the consideration of the Sefiroth.

7. Except for the Sabbath the Hebrew days of the week have never been given names and are designated by number, as they are listed here. Perhaps this was because other nations related the names to astrological deities, on whom the Hebrews frowned. These days also have been taken by some to represent the days of creation in the Bible.

It should be noted that the seven gateways of the person are all openings in the skull. No doubt this reflects the significance given to the sevens by the author as compared with the twelves which refer to organs throughout the body. However, with the exception of the eyes, the head openings are also listed in the last chapter as reflecting the love-hate, life-death characteristics of the twelve.

Varying orders are given for the seven qualities, planets, and head openings, and their significance is discussed in the later commentary on the seven. The order of the letters and the days of the week are uniform.

15. The *sabbatical year* refers to the seventh year in which the land remains fallow. The jubilee is the fiftieth year during which the land remains untilled, slaves are freed and land is returned to its former alienated owners.

Although the impact of the sevens is universal, it still is limited to the domain *under the heavens.*

16. The total number of houses evidently reflects all possible combinations of two to seven letters. The total of houses for any given number of stones is always equal to the product of that number by the total for the preceding number.

CHAPTER V
THE LAW OF TWELVE

1. Twelve simple letters ק צ ע ס נ ל י ט ח ז ו ה their foundation is sight, hearing, smell, speech, eating, coition, work, walking, anger, laughing, thought, sleep.

2. Twelve simples: they are measured by the twelve diagonal boundaries: northeast boundary, southeast boundary, high east boundary, low east boundary, high north boundary, low north boundary, southwest boundary, northwest boundary, high west boundary, low west boundary, high south boundary, low south boundary. And they widen and continue unto eternity. They are the arms of the universe.

3. Twelve simples ק צ ע ס נ ל י ט ח ז ו ה: He ordained them, hewed them, combined them, weighed them, and interchanged them. He created with them twelve constellations in the universe, twelve months in the year, and twelve chief organs in the male and female person.

4. Twelve constellations in the universe: Aries, Taurus, Gemini, Cancer, Leo, Virgo, Libra, Scorpio, Sagittarius, Capricorn, Aquarius, Pisces. Twelve months in the year: *Nisan, Iyar, Sivan, Tamuz, Av, Elul, Tishre, Marcheshvan, Kislev, Teveth, Shevat, Adar.* Twelve leaders in the male and female person: two hands, two feet, two kidneys, spleen, liver, gall-bladder, small intestine, stomach, large intestine.

5. He enthroned the letter ה in sight, bound a crown upon it, and fused them together. He created with them Aries in the universe, *Nisan* in the year, and the right hand in the male and female person.

6. He enthroned the letter ו in hearing, bound a crown upon it, and fused them together. He created with them Taurus in the universe, *Iyar* in the year, and the left hand in the male and female person.

7. He enthroned the letter ז in smell, bound a crown upon it, and fused them together. He created with them Gemini in the universe, *Sivan* in the year, and the right foot in the male and female person.

8. He enthroned the letter ח in speech, bound a crown upon it, and fused them together. He created with them Cancer in the universe, *Tamuz* in the year, and the left foot in the male and female person.

9. He enthroned the letter ט in eating, bound a crown upon it, and fused them together. He created with them Leo in the universe, *Av* in the year, and the right kidney in the male and female person.

10. He enthroned the letter י in coition, bound a crown upon it, and fused them together. He created with them Virgo in the universe, *Elul* in the year, and the left kidney in the male and female person.

11. He enthroned the letter ל in work, bound a crown upon it, and fused them together. He created with them Libra in the universe, *Tishre* in the year, and the liver in the male and female person.

12. He enthroned the letter נ in walking, bound a crown upon it, and fused them together. He created with them Scorpio in the universe, *Marcheshvan* in the year, and the spleen in the male and female person.

13. He enthroned the letter ס in anger, bound a crown upon it, and fused them together. He created with them Sagittarius in the universe, *Kislev* in the year, and the gall-bladder in the male and female person.

14. He enthroned the letter ע in laughing, bound a crown upon it, and fused them together. He created with them Capricorn in the universe, *Teveth* in the year, and the large intestine in the male and female person.

15. He enthroned the letter צ in thought, bound a crown upon it, and fused them together. He created with them Aquarius in the universe, *Shevat* in the year, and the stomach in the male and female person.

16. He enthroned the letter ק in sleep, bound a crown upon it, and fused them together. He created with them Pisces in the universe, *Adar* in the year, and the small intestine in the male and female person.

17. He made them for strife; He arrayed them as for battle. God set one against the other.

LANGUAGE NOTES

VERSE

1. The first six of these letters consist of the fifth through the tenth letters of the alphabet, consecutively. In the preceding chapter, the first three of the seven letters were the second, third, and fourth letters of the alphabet. Together with the letter A (א), which is the first letter of the three letters in chapter III, the initial groupings of all three classes form one continuous sequence of ten. This is the number of the Sefiroth and cannot be a coincidence.

The order of the functions has two principal varieties, one starting with sight, the other with wisdom. See later chapter on the twelve.

2. *Diagonal* can be translated as "oblique." The Hebrew *Alachson* (אֲלַכְסוֹן) is of Greek derivation. There are two variants of the order of the directions, discussed in the chapter on directions. It should be borne in mind that three dimensions are involved here, since high and low are added to the four cardinal directions. There is a traditional cube of space in which each edge of the cube corresponds to one of the diagonal directions. However, the statement that they widen and continue and are the arms of the universe does not seem to indicate a sealed cube but a system of polar coordinates going out from a center.

3. The Hebrew word for *constellation* is *Mazal* (מַזָל), which means "fate" or "good luck" in current usage.

4. This is not the present sequence of the Hebrew months which starts in the fall. It is an alternate sequence commencing in the spring and was probably associated with the priestly sect. This arrangement parallels that of the Zodiac, which also traditionally begins with the spring. However, it was only during a particular period early in the Christian era that the constellations of the Zodiac corresponded to the seasons and therefore to this list of months. See later chapter on the twelve.

The author calls these organs of the body *leaders* (*Manhigim* מַנְהִיגִים). Similarly, he says in the last chapter that the twelve letters lead the constellations. The twelve organs seem to have only a limited application to the twelve functions. In fact, a number of the functions can be directly linked with the seven openings of the head, which include four of the five traditional senses. The words translated here as *small* and *large intestines* are obscure in their reference to the human digestive system.

15. The Hebrew *Hirhoor* (הִרְהוּר), translated here as *thought,* also means "meditation" and is a doubling of the original root which means "to conceive," i.e. in the mind (*Haro* הָרֹה).

17. The theme that the twelve are made for warfare is further expounded upon in the last chapter, where four triads are envisioned, two sets of two opposite triads each. This is reminiscent of the Ptolemaic classification of the signs of the Zodiac. See later chapter on the twelve.

CHAPTER VI

THE THREE LAWS

1. Three mothers אמש From them came forth
three fathers: fire, air, and water, and from the fathers
came offspring. Three fathers with their offspring, seven
planets with their hosts, and twelve diagonal boundaries.

2. They are attested to by faithful witnesses in the
universe, the year, and the person: the laws of twelve,
seven, and three embodied in the dragon, the wheel, and
the heart.

3. The three are fire, water, and air: fire above,
water below, and air ordained to balance the two. A sign
of it is that fire carries water.

4. The dragon in the universe is like a king on his
throne. The wheel in the year is like a king in a province.
The heart in a person is like a king at war.

5. God hath set every desire against another: good
against evil and evil against good. Good comes from
good, evil from evil. The good sets off the evil and the
evil sets off the good. Good is reserved for the good and
evil is reserved for the evil.

6. Three, each of which stands by itself: one has
merit, one is defective, and one balances the other two.

7. Seven divided three against three, with the one
balancing the others.

8. Twelve are at war: three love, three hate, three
give life, and three destroy.

9. The three that love are the heart and the ears.
The three that hate are the liver, the gall-bladder, and the
tongue. The three that give life are the two nostrils and
the spleen. The three that destroy are the two openings
of the body and the mouth. And God the faithful king
rules over them all eternally from his holy dwelling-
place.

10. One upon three, three upon seven, seven upon
twelve, and all adhere closely to one another.

11. These are the twenty-two letters with which I
AM, GOD, THE GOD OF HOSTS, ALMIGHTY GOD, THE
GOD OF GODS, ordained. He made of them three numerations, created from them His whole universe, and created with them the whole creation and everything to be
created in the future.

12. And when our father Abraham kept watch, and looked, and saw, and searched, and understood, and ordained, and hewed, and combined, and created, succeeding by himself, then there appeared to him the Lord of all, who took him to His bosom, kissed him on the head, called him His friend, and made a covenant with him and his seed.

13. And He made a covenant with him between the ten fingers of his feet, which is the covenant of circumcision, and between the fingers of his hands, which is the covenant of the tongue.

14. He bound the twenty-two letters on his tongue and revealed to him their foundation. He soaked them in water, He burned them in fire, He rustled them in the air. He illuminated them in the seven planets, He made them lead the twelve constellations.

LANGUAGE NOTES

VERSE

2. The *dragon* is the embodiment of the three laws operating in the universe, described in verse 4 as *like a king on his throne.* The throne could appropriately represent the celestial north pole, around which the constellation Draco, the dragon, was wound like a serpent. Due to the precession of the equinoxes, this constellation is no longer centered around the ancient pole star. Another interpretation for the Hebrew word translated as *dragon* is that it represents the line joining the constellation's head and tail, the points at which the orbit of the moon intersects the path of the sun. This line is considered to be the axis of the universe. A third interpretation extends the concept of the dragon to the whole belt of the Zodiac, in accordance with certain traditions. The Hebrew word for dragon (*Thali* תְּלִי) also means "hanging," which may suggest the Zodiac. This word resembles in sound the Hebrew word for Aries (*Taleh* טָלֶה), and Aquarius, (*Dli* דְּלִי).

The *wheel* is the embodiment of the three laws operating in the year, or in time, described in verse 4 as *like a king in a province.* This is the revolution of the wheel of the Zodiac which originated, no doubt, as a calendar to indicate the divisions of the year. It is the king travelling abroad, or the path of the sun.

The *heart* is the embodiment of the three operating in man, described in verse 4 as *like a king at war.*

5. Man is the scene of the struggle of all his inclinations against one another.

8. In chapter II, the body houses twenty-two inclinations. Here the law of the twelve is pictured as the embodiment of war.

9. The *heart,* which was represented above as the king at war, is now represented as one of the three that love in the war of the twelve. But all twelve are ruled over by God the King.

10. The three laws rest upon one another and all upon the one unity.

12. Abraham repeats all the steps in creation after he takes the initial preparatory steps, and he "succeeds by himself." All the authorities seem to agree that this paragraph is a later interpolation.

THE FOUR ELEMENTS
AND THE LAW OF THREE

THE FOUR ELEMENTARY SUBSTANCES of the *Book of Creation* — spirit, air, water, and fire — are quite different from the usual interpretation of the superficially similar Greek elements — fire, air, water, and earth. The first important difference is that the elements of our author are not really separate. They are bound in unity by spirit, which underlies and gives rise to the other three.

The Western world prides itself that its own discovery of the unity of matter — initially in the form of atoms and the chemical elements — nullified the traditional Greek idea of the elements. But the theory of atoms was also formulated first by the ancient Greeks. Most of their philosophical schools believed in a primary substance which was variously air, fire, water, or ether, from which the other elements were derived by rarefaction and condensation. Furthermore, their doctrine of *pneuma* combined the connotations of air or breath with spirit, in a manner reminiscent of the close relationship between the two which prevails in the *Book of Creation.*

This ambivalent use of one word to unite the subtle corporeality of breath with spirituality is to be found in other religious currents as well, and there is no reason to think that our author was insulated from them. In the *Book of Creation,* the first element derived from spirit is also called spirit, or air of spirit. Finally, it is called air when it is applied to the created world. This spiritual air is rendered as "ether" by some translators. Actually, the Hebrew word here used for spirit, *Ruach* (רוּח), as in Genesis, actually means "wind," and therefore derivatively breath. The word used for air, *Avir* (אֲוִיר), sometimes in combination with the word for spirit, means atmosphere or space and appears to be philologically related to the word for light, *Aur* (אוֹר).

The second significant difference between the scheme of the *Book of Creation* and our traditional scheme is that earth is not an original element in the former, but only derivative from water. It represents the water-element in the spatial universe, just as heaven represents the fire-element. In effect, earth appears only when the elements encounter the physical universe. Earth is the solidification of the water element and is therefore said to come from snow, frozen water, and to appear first as mud, liquid earth.

Thus the *Book of Creation* starts with a tri-partite division, a law of three reminiscent of the Hindu, Egyptian, and Sumerian cosmogonies, and bearing fruit in the trinities of the later Kabbalah's Sefirothic Tree of Life.

Air, derived from spirit, balances heaven and earth in the universe. Its season of moist abundance balances, in time, the seasons of heat reflecting the fire-element, and of cold reflecting the water-element. But most important, the air element in man represents his body as a whole (*Geviyah* גְוִיָּה) or the trunk, its central part. It balances his head and belly, his fire and water. And to emphasize the role of the balancing element as a building block of the universe, the author indicates that great concrete pillars are hewn from intangible air, substance from the void.

The third significant difference between the *Book of Creation* and other cosmogonies is the relative position of the water and fire elements. Our author, following the primacy of water in Middle Eastern schemes, in the first chapter derives water from air and fire from water. But in the last chapter he gives the puzzling illustration that fire, which is above and sibilant, carries water, which is below and silent. It is doubly puzzling because the angels and God's dwelling, including His throne of glory, are formed from fire.

This preeminent position of fire appears in many traditions, notably Hindu and Iranian, and it is not lacking in Egypt and among the Greek philosophers, as well. It is embodied in the sun and before that in the gods of the sky. It gives both light and heat and has come to represent the lowest realms of the nether world as well as the highest realms of the empyrean.

In Genesis, light is separated from darkness on the first day of creation, but the waters are there before creation for the Spirit of God to move upon. The sun, moon, and stars are not created until the fourth day, and before that God has already separated the lower from the higher waters.

So these two elements appear on different levels. The higher fire is actually identified in some quarters with spirit or its first emanation, the air of spirit, as the active masculine element, whose tendency is always upward. The higher waters represent the feminine formless potentiality whose center of gravity is downward, and from which all is born.

The *Zohar* of the later Kabbalah will visualize the creation of the world as a fall of the light of the upper world into the formless waters of the lower, creating an inversion of the normal hierarchy of elements. Some such inversion is no doubt at work in the cosmogony of the *Book of Creation.* It is evident even in the fact that air, the balancing element between water and fire, is not created afterward to balance them but before them, in a timeless birth and equilibrium.

Finally, as must already have become evident, the *Book of Creation* is not describing elements as we know them. Even Empedocles, who is regarded as having originated the notion in the fifth century B.C., did not think of his four elements as material, but gave them the names of gods. He called them the "roots" of matter, its most universal forms. They were the qualities of hot, cold, moist, and dry made into elements.

In the *Book of Creation* the qualities of temperature and moisture make their appearance in the world of time as mother letters, just as the elements are their appearance in the spatial universe.

But our author again makes it clear that the most important correspondences are to the person of man. When he localizes fire, water, and air in the human head, abdomen, and trunk, it becomes obvious that he is referring to a method of salvation which becomes effective by uniting man's separate parts, just as the elements have their unity in spirit. Its first descendant, air, harmonizes head and abdomen, fire and water, heaven and earth. The differences among the elements symbolize the variations in man's makeup, which in turn reflect the diversity of the cosmos.

THE LAW OF SEVEN

THE AUTHOR'S STATEMENT that the creator loves sevens throughout the universe echoes the high regard for
that number throughout the ancient world. Pythagoras
had based music on the harmonic ratios of seven different notes which he considered as corresponding to the
"harmony of the spheres." He had also interpreted the
universe in terms of opposing qualities.

The *Book of Creation* bases its law of seven on the
seven double letters. These letters can be pronounced in
opposite ways, becoming either soft or hard by the presence or absence of a dot in their center. Because of this,
they symbolize the dualistic nature of the world — each
representing a twofold quality.

The idea that life has meaning only in relation to
death, beauty in relation to ugliness, etc. is a fundamental conclusion about the polar nature of reality. The
seven opposing qualities are reflected in the character of
the seven planets known to the ancients. Some regarded
the planetary worlds as entirely evil in contrast to the
stars. Others regarded the planets as either beneficial or
maleficent, just as the seven Hebrew letters had two
aspects. This concept of the varying character of the
planets has come down to modern astrology.

Apart from each of the seven letters, planets, and
qualities having this Janus-like nature, opposition is built
into the sequence of seven itself. It is structured from
two opposing units of three, harmonized by a common
center. We may deduce that the law of three serves as a
foundation for the law of seven, just as both of them will
be used to construct the law of twelve. All are based on
the harmony of opposition.

Thus, the six directions North-South, East-West,
and Up-Down consist of three two-faced dimensions, to
which the author adds their divine center as balance. He
makes space, which may also be interpreted as time, an
essential constituent of the material world spelled out by
the ten Sefiroth, in an ultramodern anticipation of recent
thought.

Similarly, the head has three pairs of openings, the
eyes, ears, and nostrils, which seem to be interpreted by
the author as kept in balance by the mouth. Its tongue,
that is, speech, is also in Hebrew the pointer or balance of

the scale, to which he compares the law of three. On their negative side, however, the tongue can hate and the mouth destroy as part of the law of twelve in chapter VI. What is notable about the correspondence of the seven with the human body is that their analogues are all in the head. They are described as gates or openings and are evidently the gates of the senses, so that the law of seven refers to the world of the senses.

The reflection of this law as a system of balance in the planetary world is even more difficult to interpret because there are at least three orders in which the planets are tiven in various versions of the *Book of Creation*.

The dominant order given is exactly that of the pre-Copernican system, espoused in the second century A.D. by the Alexandrian Greek Astronomer Ptolemy: Saturn, Jupiter, Mars, Sun, Venus, Mercury, Moon. The sun and the moon are included among the planets revolving around the earth, since the earth was not conceived of then as a planet.

The two groups of three planets on either side of the central sun are called the major planets and the minor planets respectively, and actually are separated by a group of asteroids. It is obvious that this arrangement with the sun in the center corresponds to the *Book of Creation's* law of seven, the two groups of three with a common center.

This actually is the order of positions observed from the earth, as well as their arrangement according to the period of planetary orbits. In this order, the sun appears to be in the position actually occupied by the earth, appearing to revolve around it with the other planets. It is well known that the actual geographic centrality of the sun was propounded by Aristarchus several centuries B.C., although it was not accepted until Copernicus in the sixteenth century A.D.

Could this be, in part, because the Ptolemaic symbolism of man's centrality on the earth, as a potential image of the divine, was considered more important than the technicality of the sun's spatial centrality? God, as symbolized by the sun, was more closely linked with man in His Ptolemaic position in the midst of the planets circulating around man on the earth than in His far-off Copernican grandeur, with everything circulating around Him as the sun.

There was another eason why the Ptolemaic system made more sense for the ancients. They were well aware of the vast horizon of stars and some had divided the universe as a whole into seven worlds, ascending from the lowliest of matter to the Deity. The Ptolemaic scheme could be a shorthand symbol for the whole system, each of its planets symbolizing an entire level of worlds or galaxies. The moon would be the newly formed outcrop of matter, while Saturn, the Roman form of the Greek god Cronos, points in the direction of the Deity. Uranus, Neptune, and Pluto were not included in the ancient scheme of planets because they were not visible to the naked eye and their existence was confirmed only in recent centuries.

There are other orders given for the planets in textual variations of the *Book of Creation*. One of the most significant is that in which the order is completely reversed, the positions of the sun and the moon likewise reversed. This is reminiscent of the interchange between the elements fire and water referred to in the preceding chapter. The moon has always been associated with the feminine element water, and the sun, of course, with the masculine fire.

In the ancient Mesopotamian Near East, the Mother Goddess, associated with the fertility of the earth, was the dominant deity, although the gods associated with the heavens, the air, and the waters (parallel to the three elements of the *Book of Creation*) exercised a limited jurisdiction over their realms. In Egypt, on the other hand, the male king and a male god were dominant. Associated with these two emphases were the lunar month in the Mesopotamian calendar and the solar year in the Egyptian.

The emphasis of the Judaic God was definitely patriarchal, although the feminine element remained, for example, in the Shekhinah (the presence of God), the Sabbath, the soul, and the mythology of the goddess Lilith. Whether this masculine emphasis was imported from Egypt or was a result of the domestication of animals (Abraham's wealth was in flocks of animals), the Hebrews were forced by the vagaries of the seasons to adjust their originally lunar calendar to a luni-solar one. Nevertheless, there were those among the Hebrews who prided themselves on being the guardians of a special tradition and who observed a strictly solar calendar. Among them were the sect associated with the Dead Sea Scrolls and the authors of the *Book of Jubilees* and the *Book of Enoch*.

They began their week on the fourth day of the regular week. This is of interest because, as we have seen, the fourth is the central position in the order of the planets, as in the corresponding days of the week of the *Book of Creation*. The Bible states that God created the sun on the fourth day, which corresponds to its central position in the Ptolemaic scheme.

Our current order of days, whose names are based on the Teutonic equivalents of the Roman-Greek-Babylonian planetary gods, is derived from the Ptolemaic scheme through an intricate astrological symbolism. The first hour of every day was considered to dominate that day. If we start with Sunday and follow the Ptolemaic order, then the first hour of the next day will be ruled by the moon, for whom Monday is named. In this way we derive the order Sun, Moon, Mars, Mercury, Jupiter, Venus, and Saturn, to which correspond the Saxon Sun, Moon, Tiw, Woden, Thor, Frigg, and Saterne. The last day becomes Saturday, the Biblical seventh day of rest. When the Roman Emperor Constantine made Christianity the state religion in the fourth century, he also adopted the seven-day week as part of the calendar. However, the *Book of Creation* follows the Hebrew tradition of not listing names for the days of the week but only numbers, corresponding to the days of creation.

As with the planets, there are at least two orders given for the corresponding seven qualities. One list begins with wisdom, its fourth and central member being life. The second order, given here, is the more frequently used, and begins with life, as if it were starting in the fourth and middle position of the first list. Life is the solar influence referred to above; its position corresponds to that of the sun which appears in two varying dominant positions. In the first list, corresponding to the Ptolemaic scheme, it can be viewed as supporting the temporal process at its midpoint, as the permanent balance for an eternal process. In the second list, it is the initiating or creative influence in a process consumed in time.

While life, symbolized by the sun, has this dominant position in the process of development, wisdom, which heads one of the two lists, was universally regarded in the ancient world as the prime mover beyond the process. It was called by the Babylonians the god who resided in the "deep," by the Hindus the father of creation, by the Greeks and Gnostics, *Sophia,* mistress of the created universe. It pervaded the Biblical wisdom literatures and ended in the later Kabbalah as *Chokmah,* the immediate offspring of the Diety.

An example of the regard with which the Hebrews viewed the number seven can be found in Proverbs IX:1, 'Wisdom hath builded her house, she hath hewn out her seven pillars." The "Seven Spirits of God" also make their appearance in the Revelation of St. John in New Testament times.

However, for the most specific antecedent of our seven qualities we must go the source which had a profound effect on Judaism as a result of the Babylonian exile. The Persians conquered the Babylonians and inherited from them the exiled Jews, to whom they bequeathed their dualism of light and darkness or good and evil, their angelology, and their doctrine of resurrection.

This dualism was personified in the conflict between good and evil spirits symbolized in the *Book of Creation* by the seven pairs of opposites. At the same time, we must remember that these seven themselves consisted of the three pairs united by a center.

The supreme being in the Iranian-Zoroastrian scheme, Ahura Mazda "the Wise Lord," had six spirits or entities that accompanied him. They seem to have been grouped into the three functions of Sovereignty or Dominion, War, and Fecundity, but to have involved as well the other qualities on our list. These Holy Spirits, appearing here as functions of society, were related to archangels and to gods, Hindu as well as Iranian. However, they also corresponded to social classes, to material elements, to psychological faculties, and to the progress of the soul through the seven planetary spheres. The material elements of which the "Holy Immortal Ones" were patrons included in a dominant position those involved in the law of three of the *Book of Creation*. This further emphasizes for us the relationship of the two laws of seven and three. One of the fundamental elements in the Iranian scheme is the ox, which is the meaning of the Hebrew word *Aleph,* the predominant and balancing element in the law of three. Much of the above scheme was subsequently taken over and elaborated by the sects known collectively as the Gnostics.

THE LAW OF TWELVE

THE NUMBER TWELVE was very widely used in the ancient world, primarily because it reflects the number of lunar circuits or months in a solar circuit or year. No doubt the twelve divisions of the Zodiac originated from this division of time, although the signs themselves had more complicated origins.

The *Book of Creation* draws this parallel between the Hebrew months and the signs of the Zodiac and extends the correspondence as well to man's psychic functions, parts of the body, spatial directions, and the simple letters.

The names of the Hebrew months are derived from Early Babylonian. Their origins seem to be agricultural, as were the origins of the four Canaanite months mentioned in the Bible. During the period dominated by the priests before the Babylonian exile, only numbers were used for months. We have already seen that the religious influence prescribed the use of numbers for the days of the week, as opposed to the names of the planetary deities used in other countries.

But although our author employs the Babylonian month-names still in use today, he does not locate the New Year in the fall month of *Tishri* as is done today. The fall New Year is in accordance with the ancient Gezer calendar, with the calendar of the early monarchy, and was adopted following the Babylonian exile as the agricultural New Year. The *Book of Creation* lists the spring month of *Nisan* first. The spring New Year follows the priestly calendar in effect from the end of the monarchy to the Babylonian exile. It seems to be associated with the solar, Egyptian influence reflected in the Apocrypha.

The adoption by the author of the spring New Year makes possible the parallel with the Zodiac, which commences with the sign of Aries, the Ram, traditionally associated with the spring equinox. However, this does not take into account the phenomenon known as the precession of the equinoxes. The latter has ensured that the constellation of Aries has not fallen in the spring equinox, i.e. corresponded with our author's spring month of *Nisan* as the New Year, since about the second

century A.D. This fact is considered by some to date the
Book of Creation.

The coincidence of the spring equinox with Taurus
the Bull, the sign-constellation preceding Aries by 2000
years, may have actually marked the founding of the
Zodiac and the mapping of the constellations. Authorities point to the fact that Taurus represented the
spring equinox in the ancient Middle East and to the
universal worship of the bull during the third millenium
B.C. It may have left its mark on the Hebrew alphabet in
the first letter *Aleph,* meaning "ox," possibly resembling
an ox in its shape. Also, the last letter *Tau,* meaning "the
sign," is the first letter of the Hebrew word for bull, *Taur*
(תּוֹר).

In any case, the second century A.D. may represent
the end of the age in which Aries was the spring month.
The beginning of that age, during which Aries
corresponded with *Nisan,* as in the *Book of Creation,*
would have occurred much earlier.

Unlike the Hebrew months, which were purely
Babylonian in origin, the signs of the Zodiac, with which
they are correlated in the *Book of Creation,* appear to have
had a mixed origin. Although Assyrian astronomers
standardized the Zodiac in the seventh century B.C.,
about half of the names of the signs and most of the signs
themselves seem to come from Egyptian hieroglyphics.
Nevertheless, they were undoubtedly available to the
author of the *Book of Creation* in their already
standardized form.

The second century astronomer Ptolemy also sys-
tematized a classification of the twelve signs of the
Zodiac, relating them to the four elements and to the
three qualities of existence. The four elements are themselves related to the hot-cold, dry-wet characteristics,
each being a different combination. Earth, for example, is
cold-dry, while air is hot-wet. The three qualities of
existence are called cardinal, fixed, and mutable and are
somewhat similar to the three qualities of Hinduism:
ascending, descending, and energetic.

This classification was retained in the subsequent
development of astrology which, among other develop-
ments, used it to group the signs into three sets of four

contrasting elements or into four sets of three contrasting levels of qualities. But the *Book of Creation,* assuming it was post-Ptolemaic, does not attempt to give any further significance to the signs. This may be simply in keeping with the character of the book as an outline of correspondences and basic structures. On the other hand, it may be an acknowledgement of the basic prejudice of Hebrew thought against imputing excessive astrological efficacy although accepting the Zodiac as a measure of time and season.

Nevertheless, we have already seen the temperature-moisture theme as reflecting the law of three in time. This law itself appears to be strictly analogous to the three qualities of existence imputed by Ptolemy to the Zodiac and by Hinduism to the universe. It also serves the *Book of Creation* for the derivation of the four elements. Furthermore, the author classifies the law of twelve as four groups of three warring against one another. He states that the law of twelve is based on the law of seven, which is based on the law of three.

The seven consist of two threes with a central element. If we eliminate the central element, then the resultant six matched by another opposite six will result in twelve at war. An example of this is the way in which the seven planets are considered in astrology to "rule" the twelve signs, the sun and moon ruling one house each and the planets two each.

The *Book of Creation* also exhibits or implies other inter-relationships among its three laws. As far as the directions are concerned there is a simple mathematical progression from the three axes to the six dimensions, which are their extensions, plus a central dimension, making seven; to the twelve diagonal dimensions, which are combinations of the six.

The attempt to interrelate the three laws becomes fascinating in the final chapter's synthesis of the parts of the body. Here the essence of the law of twelve is revealed as a state of war between four groups of three: the forces of love versus hate and the partisans of life versus death. Representing love are the heart and the ears; representing life are the nostrils and the spleen.

This characteristically subdued analysis conceals

themes of the highest significance. The heart, traditionally the center and unity of the individual, was not mentioned before this last-chapter synthesis. The ears, atten-
tive in their function of listening, reach out like the heart
in a unifying gesture of love. The nostrils convey life
through the breath, while the spleen guards and defends
it.

Interesting also is the hitherto unrevealed destruc-
tive side of the tongue in hate and of the mouth in death.
The tongue was earlier regarded as a harmonizing influence in the law of three and the mouth as a central organ
among the senses in the law of seven.

With its emphasis on internal and sense organs, the
Book of Creation differs quite markedly from other ancient lists such as those of the Hindus and Romans, which
relate the signs of the Zodiac to outer parts of the body.
Even the later Kabbalah emphasizes the correspondence
of the ten Sefiroth to the external bodily form. It would
appear that the author had access to medical information
available only before the second century A.D. in Alexan-
dria, when the practice of vivisection ceased.

There are two variant lists of the twelve human
functions and the twelve bodily parts. The list of human
functions used here starts with sight and has as its fourth
member speech. The second list starts with speech and
has sight as its fourth function. The list of bodily parts
used here starts with the right hand. However, in the
variant list, the right hand is the fourth member, which
again emphasizes the relationship between first and
fourth.

We previously have encountered this tendency to
start anew at the fourth place, the central position in the
law of seven. It can be regarded as another creative
beginning after the completion of one law of three,
thereby interchangeable with the first position. In the
planetary scheme these positions were usually occupied
by the sun or moon, or by Saturn representing the deity.

We have seen that this relatedness of fourth and first
was also built into the structure of the Zodiac by
Ptolemy, who arranged the twelve constellations into
three successive sets of four. Here there is no need for

outer variation in the order of the constellations to demonstrate the law of three, as with the planets. In fact, the sphere of the fixed stars was not to be tampered with, since it was closest to the realm of the deity, while the orbits of the planets were the domain of the temperamental inferior gods or angels.

It would appear that the Hebrews never lost their astrological perspective and used its symbols as did all the other heirs of Mesopotamian astrology. Many ancient synagogues and some modern ones weaved the Zodiac into their design. Some of the mosaics included the sun and moon as well.

There were other Biblical examples of the number twelve which became allied to the Zodiac but were not mentioned in the *Book of Creation*. Jacob blessed his twelve sons, comparing five of them to symbolical animals, some reminiscent of the signs of the Zodiac. They gave rise to twelve tribes geographically arranged in accordance with the cardinal directions and identified by many with the Zodiac. The twelve stones in the breastplate of the High Priest were arranged in four rows of three each, interpreted as reflecting three signs of the Zodiac in each season.

The astrological interpretation of these Biblical references was often developed and magnified by the rabbinical community itself. But like our author, it always took pains to emphasize that the real God is the invisible center behind the visible cosmos.

THE TEN SEFIROTH

ALTHOUGH THE TERM *Sefiroth* can be related to "sphere," not of Hebrew derivation, and to the word for sapphire, its etymology seems obviously based on the root developed in the *Book of Creation* into the three forms of expression: counting, speaking, and writing. Counting seems the primary meaning of this three-letter root as it refers to the feminine term *Sefiroth* as well as to the kindred masculine form *Sefarim*. *Sefarim* is translated here in its usual sense of numeration, but the author broadens its meaning to encompass the three forms of expression. It follows that the Sefiroth begin by being based on number, but a very different kind of number than the arithmetical variety. They are living numbers and also numbered principles, so that the meanings of qualitative principles and living movement are added to the initial meaning of number.

These require a more flexible tool than mere numbers. This tool is at hand in that the numbers themselves are also letters, serving a dual function; and the letters, like the Sefiroth, are derived from spirit. As the *Book of Creation* makes clear, there are different series implied, for there are thirty-two paths, ten Sefiroth, and twenty-two foundation letters. Nevertheless, it also emphasizes that ten of the letters, the three mothers and the seven doubles, are parallel to the ten Sefiroth.

Some have felt that the Sefiroth represent a more ideal, archetypal world among the four worlds of the Kabbalah, while the world of the letters is the created world of matter. In any case, the Sefiroth represent a need for intermediaries between God and man, intermediaries which were not necessary when man could face God directly. They have been called the Hebrew version of emanations from God, which do not diminish Him. Unlike other schemes, they are one with Him, varying in facet and sometimes in sequence, but always organically linked in unity.

The Sefiroth of the *Book of Creation* appear as quite different from those of the later Kabbalah. Whereas the former consist of spirit, its three elements and six directions, the latter are triads of interacting qualities arranged in three columns. The law of three, which is the law of

combination of the three elements and their correspondences in the *Book of Creation,* obviously is analogous to
the triads in the later Kabbalah.

In addition, there is a correspondence between the
qualities listed for the law of the seven double letters, and
the qualities of the Sefiroth of the later Kabbalah. Wisdom appears in both lists as the Demiurge which created
the world, as it does in fact throughout the Old Testament, the Apocrypha, and most ancient traditions. At the
lower end of the two lists, Kingdom in the *Zohar* and
Dominion-Sovereignty in the *Book of Creation,* represent
the whole of the created world. Two other principles that
appear on both lists are Beauty and Fertility (Foundation
in the later Tree of Life).

The seven double letters with their corresponding
qualities are related in the *Book of Creation* to the six
directions with the holy palace in the center sustaining
them all, in chapter IV verses 3 and 4. These six directions also measure the last six Sefiroth, in chapter I verse
5. The relationship between these qualities and those of
the Sefiroth of the later Kabalah mentioned above, is
highly suggestive.

It is interesting enough that the list of the later
Kabbalah, which has had a tremendous influence on
Western thought as the Tree of Life, should have as its
precursor the apparently quite different Sefiroth of the
earlier *Book of Creation,* as well as an early Talmudic list. It
also may be closely connected, as previously noted, with
the Seven Celestial Spirits of the Persians. Zoroaster's
reform of Persian religion depersonalized the Indo-
Iranian gods into spirits named for abstract qualities, but
in the Hebrew Kabbalah the mythological, personal aspects of the abstract qualities are never too far below the
surface.

Wisdom, for example, is a divine person even in the
Old Testament. In the later Kabbalah, Understanding, as
Binah, conceals the figure of the Mother-Goddess of all
ancient religions in her higher aspect. In her lower aspect
she becomes the daughter, Kingdom-Sovereignty,
Malkuth, the *Shekhinah* or feminine aspect of the deity
exiled with the nation of Israel. Between the mother and

the daughter is the figure of the son, *Tifereth,* represented by the quality Beauty, in whom the father and mother find their perfection.

These four familial figures are construed in the later Kabbalah to embody the four letters of the Tetragrammaton, the unspoken name of God, which embodies the stages of creation. They are paralleled in the divine tetrads of many other ancient religions involving the gods of heaven, air, water, and earth. The essence of the qualitative principles is largely reducible to a deeper view of the elements which form the basis of the earlier Sefiroth, and the difference between the earlier and the later Kabbalahs, turns out to be one of emphasis and interpretation.

THE LETTERS

IN ALPHABETS SUCH as the Semitic which use one set of symbols to represent both letters and numbers, there is a basic ambiguity as to which is being indicated. There are, however, two different sets of names according to whether the same symbols are being regarded as letters or numbers. In the first chapter of the *Book of Creation* the names of the numbers are used to designate the ten Sefiroth. The names of the letters are never used in this work and the symbols standing by themselves are generally taken to represent the letters.

There is an added ambiguity in that the letter-numbers, as well as their symbols, are all called foundation letters, being elements out of which the universe was created. They are elemental letters, in the Greek sense of the term. Furthermore, they are expressed by being enumerated, spoken, or written. They are derived from spirit at the top of the hierarchy of emanations and they are its expression throughout its development.

The later Kabbalah of the Zohar regards the twenty-two letters as the pathway between the ten Sefiroth; the Book of Creation refers at its beginning to thirty-two pathways, the Sefiroth plus the letters.

The *Book of Creation* divides the letters into three sets: the three mother letters, the seven double letters, and the twelve simple letters. But again, this is not just a process of enumeration and classification. These three groups each express a different law of the universe.

The whole structure of each law seems to be hung on the characteristics of the letters composing it and projecting their correspondences to the spatio-temporal universe, to man and his body, to the ideal qualities. Nevertheless, these characteristics are elusive, especially when alternate correspondences exist for the same letters.

It is remarkable that the first ten letters of the Hebrew alphabet are divided in order, with no exceptions, among the three laws: A for the law of three; B, G, and D for the law of seven; H, V, Z, Ch, T and Y for the law of twelve. The balance of the letters are scattered in a hit or miss fashion among the three. One would almost be tempted to say that the position of the first ten letters in the three groups represents the presence of the ten

Sefiroth in the world of the letters, for the division into the three groups corresponds exactly to the natural division of the Sefiroth in the first chapter: 1, 3, and 6.

The book contains a thorough classification of the letters according to their place of pronunciation in the mouth, but this is completely unrelated to the division into three groups. Of course, the Hebrew letters are consonants only, the vowel marks not having been reduced to writing until many centuries later. Neither do the final forms of the consonant-letters play a part in the classification. The number is exactly twenty-two, not the twenty-eight of the Arabic alphabet or the twenty-four of the related Greek alphabet. The number twenty-two does correspond exactly to the number of trump cards or Major Arcana of the Tarot pack. As a result, a whole literature has grown up on the relationship of the two.

It should be noted that the later Jewish Kabbalah has not lacked its own literature on the significance of the letters. The *Zohar* itself contains the much-quoted parable of the creation of the letters. Furthermore, the development of the letters as the connecting links of the ten Sefiroth is a whole field of interpretation. Various Kabbalistic works have the alphabet as part of their titles.

This later literature brought to the fore various techniques for combining letters so as to touch a higher reality to which they were considered the key. Although the *Book of Creation* does not specify these methods of combination, it does emphasize the combination of the letters both to create words and to create the universe.

Combination is one of a series of operations on letters described in the *Book of Creation.* He ordained or decreed them by voice, He hewed them or engraved them from spirit, He combined them, He interchanged them, He weighed them, He bound a crown upon them, and enthroned or gave them dominion over their realms. The three mother letters seal the air, heaven, and earth. Similarly, the three simple letters which form the name of God seal the six directions.

The employment of the letters in these fashions is not restricted to God. They are part of the process of creation, and Abraham as well becomes capable of putting them to this use.

THE DIRECTIONS

ONE OF THE MOST puzzling of the concepts in the *Book of Creation* is its notion of spatial directions.

In the first chapter, the six directions appear deceptively simple as the last six Sefiroth, following the first four which are the elements. Immediately here, the shocking idea is encountered that man and the universe do not consist simply of elements but of their confluence in a world of extension.

God turned upward for high, downward for low, forward for east, backward for west, right for north, left for south. Each direction is thus combined with a motion which no doubt was highly significant to the author.

Together with the holy palace in their center, they correspond to the seven double letters and their analogies in space, time and man. Their significance is amplified in that they are sealed by the three letters in the name of God, *Yod He Vav,* its fourth letter being a repetition of the *He.* Each direction is sealed by a different arrangement of the three letters, conveying a different meaning. As a three-letter word root, it may be considered related to the verb "to be," in which case each variation could be a different tense or mood. Thus VYH with its direction may correspond to the future, HYV to the infinitive, HVY to the imperative.

In this way the spatial directions are reflected in time as well as in space. Furthermore, the six directions involved with their center in the law of seven grow to twelve diagonal directions when the mutual intersections of the six are considered. Here, in the law of twelve, the temporal aspect of space is even more easily recognizable. The twelve signs of the Zodiac were no doubt originally envisioned as a seasonal clock. The constellations falling at the cardinal points represent the four seasons. The Zodiacal clock also can be monthly, keeping track of the rotation of the lunar houses, and hourly, in the daily repetition of each house dominating the constellations.

The various directions have been taken to represent various qualities of existence, as well as dimensions of time. The *Book of Creation* states that the sealing of the six directions by the three-letter name of God involves as well the secret of the three mother letters. This name of

God, YHV, is not peculiar to Judaism alone. It appears as IAO in Gnosticism. IAO or IEU is the Greek for YHV, pronounced YAHU when the vowels are added. The four-letter unpronounced name of God, the Tetragrammaton, is formed by adding a second H to the name YHV. The pronunciation most widely suggested for YHVH is YAHVEH, but other sources suggest that it was pronounced very like the three-letter name until its vocalization was prohibited. It may also be noted that the suffix added to Biblical names to relate them to God is simply YAHU. Later Kabbalism has considered the position of the *Yod* (י) in the Hebrew square letters as the divine origin which later lengthens into the line of the *Vav* (ו) in its descent into the world. The *He* (ה) unifies the two. This reminds one of the three mother letters AMSh, symbolizing fire for above (Sh ש), water for below (M מ), and air for in-between (A א).

The polar axis of direction has always been taken to represent spiritual ascent and descent. The horizontal axes and plane have represented expansion and contraction on one level. When Ptolemy classified his signs of the Zodiac by quality according to this directional symbolism he also tied them to the elements. The cardinal quality referred to the constellations taken as being at the four cardinal points: Aries, Cancer, Libra, and Capricorn. They correspond to the elements fire, water, air, and earth respectively. Here one sees illustrated in the Greek Zodiac and its successors the theme of the *Book of Creation* that each point in the universe has both the quality of an element and that of a direction.

In this scheme, the cardinal points are the two solstices in the north and south and the two equinoxes in the east and west. The summer solstice is the furthest point south reached by the sun after which the days shorten, while the winter solstice is the furthest point north, after which the days lengthen. In traditions such as the Hindu, south therefore represents death and north life. There are further traditions in Islam and Zoroastrianism associating "cosmic light" with the North Pole and with the so-called High North appearing in the *Book of Creation*. High North is felt to be the origin and spiritual support of the world. The east-west directions of the equinoxes are usually associated with the dawning or ebbing of light, and therefore of life. Time also is involved in this symbolism since death is usually associated with the past and life with the future.

In addition to the cardinal points, the directions derive a symbolism from the orientation of man and God toward them. God established the directions from the way He faced. By facing forward to the east He bestowed the illumination of the divine face on it and created its relation to the light, and the inverse relation to the west. By having north on His right He established that whole symbolism which regards right as positive and left as negative.

This symbolism was systematically embodied in the Tree of Life of the later Kabbalah with its three columns of Sefiroth. The right column contains all the masculine, active, and therefore expansive forces. The Left column contains all the feminine, passive, and limiting powers. The central column is the seat of all the reconciling and equilibrating forces which correspond to the up-down or north-south axis.

The Sefirothic Tree of Life is a picture not only of the universe but also of its microcosm, man. Each Sefirah of the later Kabbalah corresponds to a part of man, bearing the same relation to his whole body as the Sefirah does to the Tree of Life.

The ten Sefiroth of the *Book of Creation* do not correspond in the same way to the body of man. They consist of two designs, one superimposed upon the other. The first four Sefiroth, the elements and their derivatives, cover the principal components of man divided into his upper, lower, and middle regions. The next six Sefiroth, the directions with their planetary, bodily, and qualitative correspondences, are superimposed as the law of seven on the elements of the law of three. Finally, the law of twelve embodied in the Zodiacal spatio-temporal clock is further superimposed on the body of man as a microcosm and on the universe as a macrocosm.

The directional scheme of the *Book of Creation* has been summarized by some as a cube of space. The axes of the cube constitute the six directions, while the intersec-

tions of each face with the others are said to constitute
the twelve additional diagonal or "oblique" directions.
However, this rectangular interpretation of the diagonal
directions does not seem to be in keeping with the
author's description of them as extending indefinitely.
Instead, it seems that they should be seen as polar coordinates extending indefinitely from a common center in
different directions.

This would be more in keeping with considering the
universe to be an infinite sphere, rather than the very
limited form of a cube. It is interesting in this respect that
the twelve-sided solid, the dodecahedron, was regarded
by both Pythagoras and Plato as the "sphere of the universe," the symbol of the whole.

THE METHOD OF SALVATION

IMPLICIT IN THE speculative doctrines of the *Book of Creation* is a method of salvation. It appears as the inverse of the doctrine of creation, for it is man ascending backward over the path from which he has come. Further implied is the revolutionary notion that man himself can participate in the creation as well as in his salvation, as did Abraham, to the degree that he can take part in the creative process.

Creation out of nothing begins with three numerations which come to fill the void: number, speech, and writing. All three are based on a common root (the Hebrew consonants SPR) because they are from a common spirit (from Latin *spirare,* to breathe) which comes like an emanation mediating between God and man.

With wisdom and clarity, by thinking and visualizing, man must ponder deeply. This deep probing seats the creator on His throne — that is — it calls Him to His proper place in man, from which He is ordinarily absent.

The letters and the energies they represent are ordained, formed, combined and interchanged, and used to seal space and time with the name of God. Abraham himself succeeds in creating by keeping watch, looking, seeing, searching, understanding, and combining the letters. No doubt there is a residual memory of magic here, for the harnessing of the energies of another world must be magical by definition. To illustrate, the *Book of Creation* emphasizes that what is material comes out of "thin" air, substance from the void, for air is the energy of the fundamental element — letter A . In a more materialistic vein, a Talmudic passage explains how two Rabbis who were familiar with the *Book of Creation* "made a calf one-third the natural size and ate it" (Sanhedrin 65b).

Similarly, the myriad impulses in man all come from one spirit, the multitude of words and their energies from one name of God. All the analogies and correspondences drawn by the *Book of Creation* between one world and another are of value simply because we can trace them to the one divine world.

The author unobtrusively calls this higher world the central place from which everything comes forth and to which it returns. To find it you must "restrain your mouth from speaking and your mind from thinking." It is the air of the spirit which balances fire and water, heaven and earth, in the law of the three. It is the holy palace in the middle of the six directions balancing the opposites of the law of seven. It is the king in his palace balancing the warlike arrangement of the law of twelve.

It operates in the microcosm of man's body, functions, and qualities, as well as in the macrocosm of the universe, time and God's attributes. Chapter III points to a man's body as a whole, his trunk, as the balance between his head and his abdomen. It is the element of air balancing fire and water. In chapter IV it can be only his mouth which is regarded as the center between his three pairs of senses — eyes, ears, and nostrils. But in the concluding chapter, it is man's heart which is identified as the king in him. Similarly, the center of time is identified as the "wheel" or Zodiac. The center of the spatial universe is its axis, through the North Pole in the constellation of the dragon. The divine presence as the center has become identical with the whole in which it is omnipresent.

Finally, the covenant of God with man is based on the observance of this center of life. The covenant of the tongue is the center between the ten fingers of the hand. The covenant of circumcision is the center between the ten fingers of the feet. In both cases, they represent the ten Sefiroth reigned over by God from His holy dwelling-place. And the covenant rests on the return to Him.